YOUR KNOWLEDGE HAS VALUE

- We will publish your bachelor's and
  master's thesis, essays and papers

- Your own eBook and book -
  sold worldwide in all relevant shops

- Earn money with each sale

Upload your text at www.GRIN.com
and publish for free

Bibliographic information published by the German National Library:

The German National Library lists this publication in the National Bibliography; detailed bibliographic data are available on the Internet at http://dnb.dnb.de .

Imprint:

Copyright © 2019 GRIN Verlag
Print and binding: Books on Demand GmbH, Norderstedt Germany
ISBN: 9783346052261

This book at GRIN:

https://www.grin.com/document/502727

Max Schmidt

UN's Sustainable Development Goals as Paradigm Change?

Deconstructing a World Consensus with (Critical) Discourse Analysis

GRIN Verlag

GRIN - Your knowledge has value

Since its foundation in 1998, GRIN has specialized in publishing academic texts by students, college teachers and other academics as e-book and printed book. The website www.grin.com is an ideal platform for presenting term papers, final papers, scientific essays, dissertations and specialist books.

Visit us on the internet:

http://www.grin.com/

http://www.facebook.com/grincom

http://www.twitter.com/grin_com

Leipzig University

Faculty of Social Sciences and Philosophy

Institute of Political Science

Literature Review

06-001-111-5 Research Module

Seminar: Application-oriented introduction to qualitative methods of political science

Summer Semester 2019

Sustainable Development Goals as Paradigm Change?
Deconstructing a World Consensus with
(Critical) Discourse Analysis – a Literature Review

Author: Max Schmidt

Study Programmes: B.A. Sociology, B.A. Political Science

Submission Date: 2019, May 30

Table of Contents

1 Introduction

In late 2015, one of the most far-reaching consensuses in the world was unanimously agreed upon by the 193 countries of the United Nations (UN) General Assembly: the Sustainable Development Goals (SDGs). Set out to fulfill ambitious development targets by 2030, ranging from the complete eradication of poverty in all its forms everywhere (Goal 1) to strengthening the Global Partnership for Sustainable Development (SD) (Goal 17), this framework is part of the so-called Post-2015 Development Agenda respectively 2030 Agenda (eponymous by the main document constituting the SDGs passed by the UN in 2015). As the intended outcome of this process, which was initiated in 2012, the SDGs are the legitimate successor of the Millenium Development Goals (MDGs), a set of eight goals that were promised to be reached by 2015 by the UN Millenium Declaration (passed in 2000). Facing manifold shortcomings of the MDGs, which were measured by a mere 18 targets, the SDGs were extended to 17 goals measured by 169 targets (UN 2015).

Unsurprisingly and especially regarding their abundance, the SDGs faced harsh critique from most diverse commentators. In one of its issues in March 2015, the internationally renowned weekly newspaper The Economist, for example, portrayed the SDGs as even worse than useless. Due to their presumably bloated nature as a "myriad of top-down targets" (The Economist 2015), they would not only distract from poverty eradication as the potentially most important goal but also overlook the importance of local contexts, ultimately resulting in "cookie-cutter development policies" (Ibid.). However, the majority of publication organs and stakeholders in the international development community did not articulate an equally harsh (and narrow) critique, as the goals of the SDGs seem difficult to contradict – at least on first glance.

Attempting to contribute to filling this research gap, in this paper I strive to provide an overview of the critical academic engagement with the SDGs. This literature review is structured as follows: Firstly, a short introduction to the key terms facilitated in this paper will be given: development and its distinction to sustainable development. Secondly, the underlying methodology of critical discourse analysis (CDA) and its differentiation from discourse analysis (DA) will be presented in order to embed the subsequent overview. Finally, before summarising this paper and giving an outlook on further research gaps, I will also briefly compare some of its main findings with the more general contribution of (C)DA to the discipline of development studies.

2 Theoretical framework

Only a few social scientific terms are as disputed as the presumable catch-all phrase development that is also occasionally called an empty signifier (Ziai 2009). Arguing from a similar point of view, Cornwall and Brock (2005) trace how the concept historically went hand in hand with other well-intended terms such as participation, empowerment or poverty reduction, ultimately resulting in a depoliticised form of one size fits all -development recipes. Its increasing depoliticisation is also stressed by Ferguson in his widely read monography *Anti-Politics-Machine* (1994). Summarising Fergusons understanding of the term, Ziai (2012, p. 4; italics by the author) states that "development is the name not only for a *value*, but also for a dominant problematic or interpretative *grid* through which the impoverished regions of the world are known to us." In this paper, although everything but exhaustive, I follow Fergusons understanding since it exceptionally demonstrates the point of reference of other development-relevant terms (e.g. under -developed, devel opment problem) and opens the etymological door for related concepts.

The term sustainable development (SD), in turn, as it was coined by the UN World Commission on Environment and Development (WCED 1987) is almost canonically understood as "development that meets the needs of the present without compromising the ability of future generations to meet their needs" and is based on the three subdimensions of social, economic and ecological sustainability. However, as it is frequently criticised (e.g. Siemiatycki 2005; Kallis 2015), SD does not represent a paradigm change regarding what counts as development and what does not – even though it stresses the responsibility of so-called developed countries (which, in contrast to the MDGs, are also affected by the SDGs). In contrast: Sachs (1997, p. 293) stresses that SD "promises nothing less than to square the circle: to identify a type of development that promotes both ecological sustainability and international justice." Sachs also notes that this definition works as an all-purpose cement, glueing both friends and foes of the concept together. Therefore and unsurprisingly, many more definitions of SD were elaborated in the last few decades, each mirroring the diverse interests among the stakeholders (Ibid.). For the sake of analysing current discourses surrounding the SDGs, however, which themselves are not provided with an explicit definition of SD, I follow the definition of the WCED (1987). I will now turn to the methodology of (C)DA in order to shed more light on how exactly the SDGs can be critically analysed.

3 Methodological framework

In the last few decades, the development discourse has progressively merged with the globalisation discourse (Ziai 2010). Against this background, one might wonder how exactly discourse can be defined in the first place. Dating back in its current understanding to the French Philosopher Michel Foucault, it is quintessentially understood as the limit of what can be said (*Feld des Sagbaren*), including strategies of denial, relativisation and de-tabooing (Jäger 2006). Moreover, every kind of communication, which is necessarily part of a specific discourse, is guided by rules and pervaded by power relations (Blatter et al. 2018). Unsurprisingly, many more criteria exist to define the nature of discourse as a social construct in its own right (e.g. Blatter et al. 2007). In this literature review, however, because of its promising applicability to discourse analysis, I follow Ziais (2010, p. 42) equally Foucault-inspired understanding of discourses as "powerful and meaningful systems of representation that interlink the production of knowledge with material practices that are in turn justified and thus substantiated."

Reconstructing a certain discourse adequately is simultaneously the object of discourse analysis (DA) as a "collective name for a number of scientific methodologies for analyzing semiosis, namely how meaning is created and communicated through written, vocal or sign language" (Cummings et al. 2017, p. 727) as well as one of its biggest difficulties (Blatter et al. 2018). Although many guidelines exist how to conduct DAs (e.g. Diaz-Bone 2006; Jäger 2006), the proposal of Hajer (2006, p. 73-74) deems most promising for DAs of policies, which the SDGs can be considered to belong to (Niklasson 2019). The proposed steps, as compiled by Hewitt (2009, p. 12), are illustrated in Table 1:

1. Desk Research – a first chronology and first reading of events
2. 'Helicopter Interviews' – to gain an overview from different perspectives
3. Document Analysis – to identify story lines and metaphors, and the sites of discursive struggle
4. Interviews with key players – to enable the researcher to construct the interviewee discourses and the shifts in recognition of alternative perspectives
5. Sites of argumentation – search the data to account for the argumentative exchange
6. Analyse for positioning effects – to show how people, institutions or nation-states get caught up in an interplay
7. Identify key incidents – to understand the discursive dynamics and the outcomes
8. Analysis of practices in particular cases of argumentation – by going back to the data to see if the meaning of what is said can be related to the practices in which it was said.
9. Interpretation – come up with an account of the discursive structures, practices, and sites of production
10. Second visit to key actors – respondents should recognise some of the hidden structures of language.

In this paper, I will mainly focus on studies facilitating critical discourse analysis (CDA). This is since, according to van Dijk (2001, p. 352), CDA is predominantly known as

a type of discourse analytical research that primarily studies the way social power abuse, dominance and inequality are enacted, reproduced and resisted by text and talk in the social and political context. With such dissident research, critical discourse analysts take explicit position, and thus want to understand, expose and ultimately to resist social inequality.

Although this definition, at least on first glance, seems to fit neatly with the SDGs own approach, the subsequent overview reveals that, proverbially spoken, all (the SDGs) that glitter is not gold. Before turning to it, and coming back to van Dijks (1998) definition, it must be stressed that CDA in distinction to DA is no method in its own right, but rather an explicitly transdisciplinary methodology (Fairclough 2012). This becomes particularly clear if one considers that its diverse disciplines of application (e.g. feminist theory, postcolonialism, cultural studies) touch upon questions of social theory rather than the more cognition-oriented DA (Keller 2011). Moreover, understood as a rather political research programme, CDA also follows different stages, starting with focussing upon a certain social wrong and concluding with identifying possible ways past the obstacles (Ibid.).

4 The status quo

In his only recently published book, *Improving the Sustainable Development Goals: Strategies and the Governance Challenge*, Niklasson (2019) stresses that academic scrutiny mostly deals with the design of the SDGs (and formerly the MDGs), with a focus on country-related reporting. Hence, they are predominantly descriptive and criticise the same only to a limited extent. Consequently, only a handful of studies conducting (C)DAs of the SDGs were published so far. Before turning to the central question – *which points of critique against the SDGs are elaborated in studies facilitating (C)DA?* – a few more words need to be said about their emergence. As Fukuda-Parr (2016), among others, points out, the SDGs most importantly address several of the MDGs shortcomings. They not only reverse the MDGs focus on the presumably desirable beliefs of simplicity, concreteness and quantification, they also set out a more transformative agenda that reflects the 21st centurys complex challenges more adequately

– ultimately resulting in the 17 goals illustrated in the appendix. Against this background, it seems fruitful to start with presenting (C)DA-based studies that analyse the emergence of the SDGs as part of the broader development framework of the UN before turning to two studies on particular SDG-issues in more detail.

Firstly, in his historical analyses of UN development policies, Protopsaltis (2017) argues that the notion of SD shares at least one crucial element with its UN-predecessors (the modernisation paradigm and the human development approach): They define inputs and outputs by quantifying targets in relation to financial resources to achieve goals of economic or human development, relying on state interventions. Hence, the author (Ibid., p. 22) derives that "using the old tools for the achievement of new goals may be due to a lack of imagination or indicate a reluctance of the UN – or the developed donor countries [...]" to critically evaluate their own understanding of development. According to Ziai (2016a) in his CDA of the key documents elaborating the MDGs, this common element of the input/output model presents the meeting development targets as a technical rather than political problem – and thereby constitutes a first storyline. The other two storylines are (1) *poverty reduction, development and growth* – which are frequently interchangeably facilitated, pointing to a focus on (Western-kind of) modernisation trajectory – and (2) *globalisation, security and development* – which point together towards a form of global economic liberalisation. Moreover, "[d]evelopment seems as a consensual, non-conflictive goal to be achieved by technical processes to which no one can object." (Ibid., p. 160) Similar to Ferguson (1994) and Kallis (2015), the author comes to the conclusion that the MDGs had a rather depoliticising character, which itself is not uncommon for UN documents, as he demonstrates by comparing the Millennium Declaration of 2000 with the UNs International Development Strategy for the Second Development Decade (1971-1980). Based on this comparison, the author notes a shift between the 1970s and 2000 towards more market-oriented measures and big push -concepts to counter poverty. However, and providing a starting point for the later SDGs, for the first time they portrayed non-economic factors and poverty reduction as their own means to economic growth (Ziai 2016a).

Rather than of discussing the continuities between the MDGs and the SDGs further, Ziai (2016b) then broadens his focus in the same monography by conducting the first historical DA of the 2030 Agenda. Most importantly, he notes that between 1949, when the former US-American president Harry S. Truman gave his inaugural address touching upon many questions of development, and 2014, when the Report of the UN High-Level-Panel on the SDGs was published, some discursive continuities remained strikingly similar. Part of them are, among others, the common credo of the harmony of objects, the problematisation of global poverty as well as the recipes of technical knowledge and economic growth (besides the dichotomy of donors and givers). According to Ziai (2016c, p. 204; italics in original), these discursive structures "can still be identified as the same structures which were used after World War II to achieve acceptance for the practices designated as *development* in a capitalist world order." However, some new issues which were not foreseeable in 1949, also took centre stage in development debates, particularly issues of sustainability, climate change and, linked to them, a higher obligation to change production and consumption patterns. Regarding the issue of poverty eradication, the author (supported by a claim of Hickel 2014) argues that, between 1985 and 2008, the World Bank substantially decreased the numbers of the severely poor by simply changing the international poverty line, a questionable practice that Apthorpe had previously criticised in 1996. This holds true even for the advanced 2010s, as Jerven (e.g. 2013; 2016) shows by indirectly suggesting the term political economy of development sta tistics.

Before turning to two CDA-based studies of particular issues within the SDGs in the next step, it deems promising to shift our attention briefly back to the well-studied transition of the MDGs into the SDGs. Briant Carant (2017), tracing this phase of evolution via a CDA, focusses on the influence of dominant economic discourses in the development paradigm, neoliberalism and Keynesianism (of which the latter was seen abandoned in the MDGs by Ziai (2016a)), in order to compare how poverty and development are constructed in particular documents. Starting from the point that diverse concerns and problem-solution frames were articulated by participants in their creation, Briant Carant (2017) also evaluates the evolutionary process by drawing two viewpoints of critique: Liberal feminist critique focused mostly of these economic discourses, whereas the World Social Forum (WSF), an annual convention that was first held in 2001 and which opposes capitalist globalisation, criticised mostly the construction of poverty within the MDGs and SDGs. While the author (Ibid.) notes that liberal feminists points of critique were particularly easily implemented in the SDGs by facilitating either of the two dominant economic frameworks, the UN failed to listen to voices such as that of the WSF (hence her papers title Unheard Voices). Although some methods were designed with the intention to consider marginalised voices, their ambitious inclusion would have been necessary to undergo a transformational shift towards a long-term, sustainable and equitable change for all. Briant Carant (2017, p. 16) sums it up:

Both the MDGs and SDGs are branded as agreed-upon documents representative of the UN as a whole. Yet the UN approach to poverty abatement is one programme among many possible. Alternative programmes also exist but critics allege that they are under-represented as a result of particular power configurations and voting patterns within the organisation.

Besides the elaboration of her own critique, the author also devotes a chapter of the same study to critically discuss the negotiation of the SDGs themselves. Most importantly, she finds striking evidence that they fail to represent the global populace targeted for development adequately. Particularly the report of the UN-Development Group *A Million Voices: The World We Want*, published in September 2013 as a summary of the consultations to formulate the SDGs, but also the polls of the UN-Website *WorldWeWant2015.org* fell short in actually allowing a million diverse voices speak. The latter even showed significant response biases, e.g. in favour of those with higher access to the internet. In addition, the low levels of voting, particularly in its second poll, can be attributed to lack of awareness and the limited access which is crucially linked to the unequal spread of NGOs and their partners. Briant Carant (2017, p. 27) strikingly captures that "the current voices represent individuals with greater levels of education who are less likely to be affected by the perils of poverty." Ultimately, the author argues, both the MDGs and the SDGs should be viewed as solely persuasive rhetoric due to their failure to adequately represent marginalised voices and their entrenchment in "power-laden hegemonic frameworks" (Ibid., p. 34).

Only one study known to the author digs deeper (in fact: at all) into the post-2015 negotiations before they were finished, i.e. before the 2030 Agenda itself was passed. This study by Brolan et al. (2015) was part of a research project to advice the European Union and discusses the notion of the right to health as part of the SDGs. Based on thematic and discourse analyses, the authors elaborate six key reasons for why the right to health was not adequately represented in the post-2015 negotiations. While three of them were related to broader issues surrounding the position of human rights within the international relations discourse, the remaining three dealt with the problem of transforming health as a human right to a single post-2015 health goal. Illustrated by this case example, but speaking more generally, Brolan et al. (2015, p. 9) arrive at the following conclusion:

Thus, rather than creating a transformative post-2015 agenda, by continuing the MDG route of divorcing rights from development goals there is real risk the post-MDG agenda will be anything but transformative – but regressively reduced to meeting basic needs, to meeting (even more) targets and sub-targets, as opposed to overcoming in-country development inequities.

Indeed, as two CDA-based studies exploring the notion of education respectively knowledge demonstrate powerfully, the SDGs follow everything but an ambitiously transformative agenda. In the first study, Brissett and Mitter (2017) examine to what extent Goal 4, "to ensure inclusive and equitable quality education for all and promote lifelong learning", promotes either a *utilitarian* or a *transformative* approach to education. The former, primarily employment-oriented focus portrays education as a "social investment designed to ensure that succeeding generations are able to assume their place as productive citizens within an established socio-economic order." (Maclure et al. 2009, p. 367) The transformative approach, in turn, "conceives the main purpose of education as addressing the inequalities and injustices that are embedded in the larger society." (Ibid.) Brisett and Mitter (2017) note that, historically, both educational transformation and utilitarianism are two dominant discourses in educational policy and practice that are both entailed in the SDGs – operationalised by the notions of SD respectively by a "neoliberal capitalist pro-growth development model." (Ibid., p. 182) Crucially, and similar to former discourses on education in the realm of development (e.g. Maclure et al. 2009), education in the SDGs is predominantly understood as a means to a utilitarian end, hence outweighing the subservient transformative approach which both must be understood as mutually exclusive (Brissett & Mitter 2017).

Consequently, following their literature review on both approaches, conducting a CDA of education under the SDGs deemed most promising to "[serve] the broader social change goal [of education]." (Ibid., p. 187) Although the SDGs seem to be more participatory, which they certainly are compared to the MDGs, their participatory emphasis remained mostly rhetorical – with a handful of major groups ultimately leading their creation process (e.g. Pingeot 2014; Ahmed 2015; Koehler 2015). Highlighting these unequal power dynamics, similar to Briant Carant (2017) and Brolan et al. (2017), Brissett and Mitter (2017) then criticise the kind of language facilitated in the SDGs as highly exclusionary and characterised by Western, scientific orientation. The very concept of goals and targets which reflects the Western obsession with action plans, as the renowned development aid sceptic William Easterly (2015) notes, might be useful in some circumstances. At the same time, however, the use of strict quantification in development policy frameworks must also be understood as overly simplistic in many ways (Hulme 2009) and is likely to marginalise certain interests and values. This is exemplified by Brissett and Mitters (2017) finding that the SDGs fail to recognise cultural differences, particularly non-Western forms of knowledge such as so-called indigenous knowledge. This might ultimately result in their contribution to limited, i.e. Western modes of thought of conceptions such as development and sustainability. Hence, it can be expected that no decision-making powers are laid in the hands of local communities – although promised at various points within the SDGs. I will come back to this point in the discussion of the second CDA-based and issue-grounded study.

The authors conclude that Goal 4 (Quality Education), conflicts with the most commonly acknowledged definition of SD by the WCED (1987), as it was presented in the second chapter of this literature review: At least four of the ten targets of Goal 4 contribute to a mostly utilitarian development discourse, for example with their focus on STEM subjects (science, technology, engineering, mathematics). Moreover, target 7 is the only target in Goal 4 that explicitly mentions SD and that provides a truly transformational approach to education, with the other five targets representing more of a mishmash of both approaches. Illustrating the conflictual power relations in the negotiation of the 2030 Agenda, Brissett and Mitter (2017, p. 199) argue that Goal 4 fails to take into account the need "of transforming curricula; adopting and validating alternative education systems and types of knowledge; or integrating environmental and/or development issues into education programs."

To be truly sustainable, they argue, the utilitarian understanding of education within the SDGs would have to be replaced by placing ecological concerns at the centre of the development discourse, equalling an ambitious turn towards a more integrative and transformative approach. Furthermore, what being truly sustainable means, is also deconstructed by Brissett and Mitter (Ibid.) in their CDA. They argue that the relationship between neoliberal economics and SD is inherently contradictory – with the SDGs trying to follow the impossible path of reconciling them. Hence, in their commitment to achieving SD through ensuring social, economic and ecological sustainability, as suggested by the language used, the SDGs themselves are highly contradictory. Similar to Goal 4, only a few more attempts to an alternative vision are presented in the SDGs, with the other 16 goals suggesting equally predominantly a pro-growth model of development – not aiming to transform the global economy at all. Consequently, the authors (Ibid., p. 193) apply Escobars (1995) critique of the

11

entire notion of SD to the SDGs by summarising them as equally "placing a premium on economic growth over the environment." Together with the consideration of their manifold contradictory goals and targets, these circumstances result in the authors plea not to have blind faith in the SDGs.

Finally, in order to illustrate the extent to which the perception of particular goals (if not the SDGs as such) can diverge from each other, a brief change of perspective seems fruitful. Briant Carant (2017), as already discussed, analyses the SDGs through a lens of dominant economic and social discourses rather than through a lens of utilitarian/transformative approaches. Regarding Goal 4, she stresses how the importance of women and girls for goal achievement is highlighted in three of the four first targets, drawing to notions of liberal feminism and Keynesianism. The author argues that this focus is further built on in target 5 which by 2030 aims to eliminate gender disparities "in education and ensure equal access to all levels of education [...] for the vulnerable, including persons with disabilities, indigenous peoples and children in vulnerable situations." (UN 2015, p. 17) While Briant Carant (2017) interprets this wording as implicit hope of increasing numbers of women in political and other previously unattainable careers, Brisett and Mitter (2017) do not shed more light on its presumably transformational potential. Instead, as they imply, this target must not be perceived as an explicitly transformative approach, but rather constitutes another target with a utilitarian end (spiced with a potentially transformative hint).

The second CDA-based study that questions the transformative potential of the SDGs, written by Cummings et al. in 2017 about the cross-cutting issue of knowledge, finds that two prior discourses of the notion of knowledge societies (KS) can be identified in the 2030 Agenda. Defined as, and referring to Faircloughs (2012) original not ion of knowledge -based economy, the notion of KS only takes a marginal position within the SDGs and can be understood as subsuming and expressing "technological discourses [...], the discourse of intellectual property, [...] of science, [...] of economic development and discourses related to the network society." (Cummings et al 2017, p. 729) Where present, they are strongly linked to a techno-scientific-economic discourse which is predominant at the level of implementation and goals and is defined by Felt et al. (2007, p. 14) as "the instrumental use of scientific knowledge for competitive economic advantage." On the level of vision and strategy, however, some elements of a pluralist-participatory discourse (PPD) are present, which can be defined as "a plural and strongly participatory vision of knowledge societies." (Mansell 2015, p. 631) Crucially, although being present in a formerly produced series of Issues Briefs in 2014 by the UN

Technical Support Team (including contributions by the Indigenous Peoples Major Group and the Farmers Major Group), the PPD was mostly excluded by the prevalent powerplay in the SDGs final elaboration: dominated by corporate interests and developed countries, an argument made by various scholars (e.g. Pingeot 2014; Ahmed 2015; Koehler, 2015; Briant Carant 2017; Brissett and Mitter 2017; Brolan et al. 2017; Cummings et al 2017).

In fact, as Cummings et al. (2017) point out by referring to Ramalingams (2015) metaphor of vessels of developing countries that are perceived to be filled with knowledge, the discourse of knowledge within the SDGs is fundamentally flawed – corresponding to concepts of developed countries. This bias is further exacerbated, considering that developing countries do not get the support they need to carry out the SDGs while also not receiving adequate policy space for carrying out their own development plans (Muchhala & Sengupta 2014). This can be understood as another indication that the SDGs mostly ignore the importance of local knowledge and development – a circumstance that undermines its own transformative agenda (Cummings et al. 2017). In fact, the only explicit reference made to traditional knowledge is associated with genetic resources in target 5 of Goal 2 (Ibid.). Being faced with the difficulty of falling short of "harness[ing] the transformational role of knowledge" (Cummings 2017, p. 22), the authors (Cummings et al. 2017, p. 737) ultimately raise the critical question: "If the SDGs do not fully represent knowledge discourses championed by technical advisers and civil society, whose discourses do they represent?"

Finally, embedding this literature review in a wider context, one might also raise the question of the contribution of (C)DA to the discipline of development studies. As we have seen, and in accordance with Ziai (2016c), the studies presented here mostly rendered material questions of poverty subservient to those of representation. Moreover, as diagnosed by the same author (Ibid.) as being typical for (C)DAs, almost no political alternatives to the points of critique were formulated by those studies. His third main point of critique can only partially be followed: Questions of agency, e.g. that of women or indigenous people, were occasionally considered. Ziais (Ibid.) last point, in turn, seems not to hold true: The studies presented here mostly tried to avoid homogenising critic against the (sustainable) development discourse into a single monolithic entity. Nevertheless, in the end it seems pertinent to adapt his (Ibid., p. 224) summary that, „[s]imply put, [the] [development] discourse wants to help the poor without hurting the rich (on a national and international level)" to the SDGs since all countries in the world are ultimately affected by them.

5 Conclusion

This paper aimed to give an overview of studies that conduct (Critical) Discourse Analyses ((C)DAs) in order to critically engage with the UNs Sustainable Development Goals (SDGs). As we have seen, only a handful of studies followed this approach by now, leaving many questions referring to the SDGs unanswered. This circumstance as well as the one that most studies conducting (C)DAs focused on the evolution of the Millennium Development Goals (MDGs) into the SDGs do not only fit with their dominant perception as a world consensus but exacerbates the difficulty of assessing the SDGs themselves appropriately. With the first targets of the SDGs promised to be reached by the end of 2020, a sharp increase in (C)DA-based studies seems necessary to raise fundamental questions: Which understanding of development, sustainable development (SD) and other key notions are presented in the 2030 Agenda, the SDGs formal framework? What are their historical trajectories and future implications?

Two of the key findings of this literature review, the lasting depoliticisation of (sustainable) development and its dominant perception as a technical problem that simply needs to be fixed, suggest that the SDGs do not equal a paradigm change within the international development community. However, compared to their predecessors, the MDGs, from which they were significantly derived, the SDGs demonstrate a selective change of mind in some realms, for example a stronger focus on issues of gender equality or climate change. Nevertheless, as two studies conducting CDAs of Goal 4 (Quality Education) (Brissett & Mitter 2017) and the cross-cutting issue of knowledge (Cummings et al. 2017) illustrate, the SDGs are characterised by some biases. Regarding education, they tend towards a *utilitarian* rather than *transformative* understanding, portraying it as a worthy social investment to increase economic growth (Brissett & Mitter 2017). Moreover, indicating their proximity to the presumably desirable development goal of knowledge societies respectively knowledge -based economies (Fairclough 2012), a techno -scientific-economic discourse of knowledge is predominant (Cummings et al. 2017).

Finally, much more light needs to be shed on questions of power configurations in the process of negotiating the SDGs. This could include, for example, a CDA of the intergovernmental Open Working Group which drafted the 17 goals later implemented by the UN General Assembly (Brolan et al. 2015). It is only by approaching the SDGs much more critically, and hence by increasing societal pressure, that they redeem their promise: improving the lives of billions of people around the world.

6 References

Ahmed, N. 2015. UN plan to save Earth is "fig leaf" for Big Business: Why the new Sustainable Development agenda is "fundamentally compromised" by corporate interests. *Medium.* 2015, September 4. [Online], available: https://medium.com/insurge-intelligence/un-plan-to-save-earth-is-fig-leaf-for-big-business-insiders-2b91c106bb03 [2019, May 21].

Apthorpe, R. 1996. Reading Development Policy and Policy Analysis: On Framing, Naming, Numbering and Coding. In R. Apthorpe and D. Gasper (eds.) *Arguing Development Policy: Frames and Discourses*. London: Frank Cass, 16-35.

Blatter, J., F. Janning and C. Wagemann. 2007. *Qualitative Politikanalyse. Eine Einführung in Forschungsansatze und Methoden*. Wiesbaden: VS Verlag für Sozialwissenschaften.

Blatter, J., P. C. Langer and C. Wagemann. 2018. Diskursanalyse. In J. Blatter, P. C. Langer and C. Wagemann (eds.) *Qualitative Methoden in der Politikwissenschaft. Eine Einführung*. Wiesbaden: Springer VS, 122-133.

Briant Carant, J. 2017. Unheard voices: a critical discourse analysis of the Millennium Development Goals evolution into the Sustainable Development Goals. *Third World Quarterly* 38:1, 16-41.

Brissett, N. and R. Mitter. 2017. For function or transformation? A critical discourse analysis of education under the Sustainable Development Goals. *Journal for Critical Education Policy Studies* 15:1, 181-204.

Brolan, C. E., P. S. Hill and G. Ooms. 2015. "Everywhere but not specifically somewhere": a qualitative study on why the right to health is not explicit in the post-2015 negotiations. *BioMed Central International Health and Human Rights* 15:22, 1-10.

Cornwall, A. and K. Brock. 2005. What do buzzwords do for development policy? A critical look at 'participation','empowerment' and 'poverty reduction'. *Third World Quarterly* 26:7, 1043-1060.

Cummings, S., B. Regeer, L. de Haan, M. Zweekhorst and J. Bunders. 2018. Critical discourse analysis of perspectives on knowledge and the knowledge society within the Sustainable Development Goals. *Development Policy Review* 36:6, 727-742.

Diaz-Bone, R. 2006. Zur Methodologisierung der Foucaultschen Diskursanalyse. *Historische Sozialforschung* 31:2, 243-274.

Easterly, W. 2015. The Trouble with the Sustainable Development Goals. *Current History.* 2015, date unknown. [Online], available: http://www.currenthistory.com/Easterly_CurrentHistory.pdfutm_content= buffer4bde9&utm_medium=social&utm_source=twitter.com&utm_campaign=buffer [2019, May 21].

Escobar, A. 1995. *Encountering Development. The Making and Unmaking of the Third World.* Princeton, NJ: Princeton University Press.

Fairclough, N. 2012. Critical Discourse Analysis. In J. P. Gee and M. Handford (eds.) *The Routledge Handbook of Discourse Analysis.* London and New York: Routledge, 9-20.

Ferguson, J. 1994. *The Anti-Politics Machine. Development, Depoliticization and Bureaucratic Power in Lesotho.* Minneapolis: University of Minnesota Press.

Felt, U., B. Wynne, M. Callon, M. E. Gonçalves, S. Jasanoff, M. Jepsen and M. Tallacchini. 2007. *Taking European knowledge society seriously. Report of the Expert Group on Science and Governance to the Science, Economy and Society Directorate, Directorate-General for Research, European Commission.* [Online], available: http://ec.europa.eu/research/science-society/document_library/pdf_06/european-knowledge-society_en.pdf [2019, May 6].

Fukuda-Parr, S. 2016. From the Millennium Development Goals to the Sustainable Development Goals: shifts in purpose, concept, and politics of global goal setting for development. *Gender & Development* 24:1, 43-52.

Hajer, M. 2006. Doing discourse analysis: coalitions, practices, meaning. In M. van den Brink and T. Metze (eds.) *Words matter in policy and planning: discourse theory and method in the social sciences*. Utrecht: KNAG/Nethur, 65-74.

Hewitt, S. 2009. Discourse Analysis and Public Policy Research. *Centre for Rural Economy Discussion Paper Series* 24. [Online], available: http://www.ncl.ac.uk/cre/publish/discussionpapers/pdfs/dp24Hewitt.pdf [2019, May 21].

Hickel, J. 2014. Exposing the great 'poverty reduction' lie. *Al Jazeera*, 2014, August 21. [Online], available: https://www.aljazeera.com/indepth/opinion/2014/08/exposing-great-poverty-reductio-201481211590729809.html [2019, May 21].

Hulme, D. 2009. The Millennium Development Goals (MDGs): A Short History of the World's Biggest Promise. *Brooks World Poverty Institute Working Paper* 100. [Online], available: https://www.law.du.edu/documents/sutton-colloquium/materials/2013/David-Hulme-BWPI-Working-Paper.pdf [2019, May 21].

Jäger, S. 2006. Diskurs und Wissen. Theoretische und methodische Aspekte einer Kritischen Diskurs- und Dispositivanalyse. In R. Keller, A. Hirseland, W. Schneider and W. Viehover (eds.) *Handbuch Sozialwissenschaftliche Diskursanalyse. Band 1: Theorien und Methoden*. 2nd edition. Wiesbaden: VS Verlag für Sozialwissenschaften, 83-114.

Jerven, M. 2013. *Poor Numbers: How We Are Misled by African Development Statistics and What to Do about It*. Ithaca and London: Cornell University Press.

Jerven, M. 2016. Research note: Africa by numbers: Reviewing the database approach to studying African economies. *African Affairs* 115/459, 432-358.

Kallis, G. 2015. 'The Degrowth Alternative'. *Great Transition Initiative*. [Online], available: https://www.greattransition.org/publication/the-degrowth-alternative [2019, May 6].

Keller, R. 2011. *Diskursforschung. Eine Einführung für SozialwissenschaftlerInnen*. Wiesbaden: VS Verlag für Sozialwissenschaften.

Koehler, G. 2015. Seven Decades of 'Development', and Now What? *Journal of International Development*, 27:6, 733-751.

Maclure, R., R. Sabbah and D. Lavan. 2009. Education and Development: The Perennial Contradictions of Policy Discourse. In P. Haslam, J. Schafer and P. Beaudet (eds.) *Introduction to International Development: Approaches, Actors, and Issues*. Oxford: Oxford University Press, 367-383.

Mansell, R. 2015. Futures of knowledge societies – destabilization in whose interest? *Information, Communication & Society* 18, 627-643.

Muchhala, B. and R. Sengupta. 2014. Means of implementation nearly toppled process of SDGs agenda. *Third World Network Info Service on UN Sustainable Development*. 2015, July 24. [Online], available: https://www.twn.my/title2/unsd/2014/unsd140705. htm [2019, May 21].

Niklasson, L. 2019. *Improving the Sustainable Development Goals. Strategies and the Governance Challenge*. London and New York: Routledge.

Pingeot, L. 2014. *Corporate influence in the Post-2015 process*. Aachen: Bischöfliches Hilfswerk MISEREOR e.V.

Protopsaltis, P. M. 2017. Deciphering UN development policies: from the modernization paradigm to the human development approach? *Third World Quarterly* 38:8, 1733-1752.

Ramalingam, B. 2015. Giving flesh to the science and innovation we need to see. *Steps-Centre*. 2015, September 24. [Online], available: http://steps-centre.org/2015/blog/giving-flesh-to-the-science-and-innovation-we-need-to-see/ [2019, May 21].

Sachs, W. 1997 The need for the home perspective. In M. Rahnema and V. Bawtree (eds.) *The Post-Development Reader*. London: Zed Books, 290-301.

Siemiatycki, E. 2005. Post-Development as a Crossroads: Towards a Real Development. *Undercurrent* 2:3, 57-61.

The Economist. 2015. *The 169 commandments*. 2015, March 26. [Online], available: https://www.economist.com/leaders/2015/03/26/the-169-commandments [2019, May 21].

Truman, H. S. 1949. *Trumans Inaugural Address*. Harry S. Truman Presidential Library & Museum 1949, January 20. [Online], available: http://www.trumanlibrary.org/whistlestop/50yr_archive/inagural20jan1949.htm [2019, May 21].

Van Dijk, T. A. 1998. Critical Discourse Analysis. In D. Tannen, D. Schiffrin and H. Hamilton (eds.) *Handbook of Discourse Analysis*. Malden, MA: Blackwell, 352-371.

United Nations. 2012. *Millennium Declaration*. [Online], available: https://www.un.org/millennium/declaration/ares552e.htm [2019, May 28].

United Nations. 2014. *A New Global Partnership: Eradicate Poverty and Transform Economies Through Sustainable Development. The Report of the High-Level Panel of Eminent Persons on the Post-2015 Development Agenda*. New York: United Nations.

United Nations. 2015. *Transforming our World: The 2030 Agenda for Sustainable Development*. New York: United Nations.

United Nations Development Group. 2013. *A Million Voices: The World We Want*. [Online], available: https://www.undp.org/content/dam/undp/library/MDG/english/UNDG_A-Million-Voices.pdf [2019, May 21].

United Nations Technical Support Team. 2014. *TST Issues Briefs: A compendium of Issues briefs prepared by the United Nations inter-agency technical support team for the United Nations General Assembly Open Working Group on Sustainable Development Goals*. [Online], available: https://sustainabledevelopment.un.org/content/

documents/ 1554TST_compendium_issues_briefs_rev1610.pdf [2019, May 21].

World Commission on Environment and Development. 1987. *Report of the World Commission on Environment and Development: Our Common Future.* [Online], available: http://www.un-documents.net/wced-ocf.htm [2019, May 21].

Ziai, A. 2009. "Development": Projects, Power, and a Poststructuralist Perspective. *Alternatives* 34:2, 183-201.

Ziai, A. 2010. From Development Discours e to the Discourse of Globalisation – Changing Forms of Knowledge about Change in North-South Relations and their Political Repercussions. *Sociologicus* 60:1, 41-70.

Ziai, A. 2012. Postcolonial perspectives on development. *Center for Development Research Working Paper Series* No. 103. Bonn: ZEF.

Ziai, A. 2016a. Millennium Development Goals: back to the future? In A. Ziai (ed.) *Development Discourse and Global History. from Colonialism to the Sustainable Development Goals.* London: Routledge, 155-172.

Ziai, A. 2016b. The post -2015 agenda and the Sustainable Development Goals: the persistence of development discourse. In A. Ziai (ed.) *Development Discourse and Global History. from Colonialism to the Sustainable Development Goals.* London: Routledge, 194-207.

Ziai, A. 2016c. Conclusion: the contribution of discourse analysis to development studies. In A. Ziai (ed.) *Development Discourse and Global History. from Colonialism to the Sustainable Development Goals.* London: Routledge, 211-235.

Appendix

Figures not included due to copyright issues.

Figure 1: *Outline of the Millennium Development Goals notable challenges.*
[Online], available: https://www.mdgmonitor.org/outline-of-the-mdgsnotable-challenges/ and https://i1.wp.com/www.mdgmonitor.org/wp-content/uploads/2015/10/MDGs-notable-challenges.png [2019, May 30].

Figure 2: *The Millennium Development Goals.* [Online], available: http://www.un.org/en/mdg/summit2010/pdf/List%20of%20MDGs%20English.pdf [2019, May 30].

Figure 3: *Sustainable Development Goals kick off with start of new year.* [Online], available: https://www.un.org/sustainabledevelopment/blog/2015/12/sustainable-development-goals-kick-off-with-start-of-new-year/ and https://i2.wp.com/www.un.org/sustainabledevelopment/wp-content/uploads/2015/12/english_SDG_17goals_poster_all_languages_with_UN_emblem_1.png [2019, May 30].

Figure 4: *Sustainable Development Goals.* (United Nations 2015, p. 16)

YOUR KNOWLEDGE HAS VALUE

- We will publish your bachelor's and
  master's thesis, essays and papers

- Your own eBook and book -
  sold worldwide in all relevant shops

- Earn money with each sale

Upload your text at www.GRIN.com
and publish for free